getting the best out of
PERFORMANCE
MANAGEMENT
in your school

Franklin Hartle, Kate Everall & Chris Baker

ACKNOWLEDGEMENTS

The self-review model based on threshold standards was jointly developed with the Royal Society of Chemistry.

Thanks to Anthony Pierce of Primary Focus for helpful contributions to the coaching and feedback sections.

The time management matrix (where will I find the time?) is adapted from a matrix in Stephen Covey, *The Seven Habits of Highly Successful People*, Simon and Schuster, London 1992.

First published in 2001

Kogan Page Limited
120 Pentonville Road
London N1 9JN

© HayGroup, 2001

British Library Cataloguing in Publication Data

A CIP record for this book is available from the British Library.

ISBN 0 7494 3637 9

Typeset by Jean Cussons Typesetting, Diss, Norfolk
Printed and bound in Great Britain by Biddles Ltd, Guildford and King's Lynn

Contents

Contents

About the authors

Franklin Hartle is Director of Education Consulting in HayGroup. In this role he is responsible for the development of all consulting business in the UK education sector. This includes work on leadership and performance management programmes for schools, further education colleges and universities. Frank has been the HayGroup project director for the Leadership Programme for serving headteachers and the Teacher Effectiveness research project for the DfEE.

He has developed a deep expertise in the field of performance management and has successfully designed and introduced performance management processes into many organisations across the world. He is the author of two books on this topic.

Prior to joining HayGroup in 1985, Frank worked as a teacher of geography in two comprehensive schools and was an Education Officer for the Cornwall and Essex local education authorities. Currently he is a governor of two schools in Essex.

HayGroup
Tel: 020 7881 7066
E-mail: Frank_Hartle@haygroup.com

Kate Everall is an experienced consultant for HayGroup. A specialist in performance management and internal communications, she works primarily in the development of management capability, in addition to advising on the design of appropriate systems. She works with both public and private sector clients including the DfEE and local government.

She has an MBA from Cranfield School of Management, and is a graduate of the Institute of Personnel and Development and a member of the International Association of Business Communicators.

Kate has a varied background. She was a negotiator and advisor in commercial property before moving into people management. Most recently she has worked with NLP (neuro-linguistic programming), and studying sports psychology and its potential links to business coaching.

HayGroup
Tel: 020 7881 7513
E-mail: Kate_Everall@haygroup.com

Chris Baker is a freelance trainer and consultant. Chris established his business, MDL, following a successful career as a chemistry teacher, as head of department and in LEA advisory work. He has been continually active in the staff development field, having helped LEAs set up their appraisal systems in the early 1990s. Chris pioneered several Investors in People support programmes, which have enabled over 200 schools to achieve the Investors in People Award.

Recently Chris worked as a lead trainer for threshold assessment and a master trainer for performance management as part of the DfEE's training programme. He produced the MDL *Guide to Threshold Assessment* and exemplar forms which were described as 'absolutely brilliant' by the schools in which they were used. He has worked extensively in schools, training teachers and team leaders to implement performance management.

Chris is a registered Ofsted inspector and manages the Royal Society of Chemistry's Professional Development Programme for teachers of chemistry.

MDL
Tel: 01606 79979
E-mail: Chris@mdl-ed.co.uk

Foreword

Schools have always managed performance. They may not have called it 'performance management', but the practice of ensuring that teachers teach what they are expected to teach and children learn what they are expected to learn is fundamental for any educational institution. Therefore, the new and more explicit emphasis on performance management is less about whether this should be done and more a matter of how it might be done – and how much is required. That is where this practical guidebook comes in.

What schools expect pupils and their teachers to achieve and how they check this achievement may not always be stated and rated explicitly. But the aims and objectives are clear, whether they are in the formal syllabuses, schemes of work, reports and policy documents, or implied in the ethos of the school and the day-to-day expectations of those involved in its management. Judgments about whether these are being achieved are made continuously and summarily by everyone involved: heads, governors, teachers, parents – even pupils.

So, performance management is not new to schools – even if some of the formal requirements to address it are. But that does not mean it is always done sufficiently well or systematically. Nor that most schools could not benefit from further clarification of what it is they are hoping to achieve, acknowledgement of successes, indications of where improvements still need to be made – and feedback on how they might be introduced.

Some may find such recognition of their success – and guidance on how more could be achieved – mostly positive and motivating. For others, assessment may seem threatening and demoralising.

The difference between these outlooks may be explained in terms of confidence: confidence in oneself and one's own capabilities, and confidence in the individuals and institutions responsible for appraising performance.

This book provides a guide not only to assessing performance, but also to managing the relationships that underpin the successful people management that is needed at the core of an effective school. It does not promulgate a 'one size fits all' solution. How could it, when there is so much variety in what schools aim to achieve and the circumstances in which they operate? But it does offer a series of tools, techniques and activities, which should help every school to improve their attention to both the quantity and the quality of children's learning. It should therefore help to develop the competence and confidence not only of those who manage schools, but also those who are managed.

Bob Doe
Editor, *The Times Educational Supplement*

Preface

> We want to improve school performance by developing the effectiveness of teachers, both as individuals and teams. The evidence is that standards rise when schools and individual teachers are clear about what they expect pupils to achieve. That is why performance management is important.
>
> (DfEE, *Model Performance Management Policy*, 2000)

The UK government has a clear agenda to raise standards of pupil attainment in schools. Its strategy is set out in the Green Paper, *Teachers Meeting the Challenge of Change* (DfEE 1998), and performance management is positioned as a key process to help raise standards. All schools in England will be operating a formal performance management process during the 2000/01 academic year. By any standards, this is an ambitious agenda. Introducing the performance management process to any organisation is never an easy task. Implementing the process in 25,000 schools to nearly 500,000 teachers in one year is a huge challenge!

This is the reason we have written this book. In my last book on performance management (Hartle 1997), I raised the question whether another book on the topic was of any value. I believed that it was then; and I think it is appropriate now. Although much has been written about performance management, and in particular teacher appraisal, I believe it is worthwhile to look more closely at the 'how' of performance management. How can it be developed into a process that adds real value? How can it be implemented in such a way that all staff are committed to it? How can it evolve into a genuine transformational process?

My view is that the rush to implement performance management in all schools within one year is creating a situation in which its potential benefits to teachers and schools might not be realised. Many performance management processes have been 'sacrificed on the altar of expediency'. In my experience, it takes from two to four years fully to implement a performance management process, and requires a significant investment in the training of all staff. In the education sector, a great deal of work needs to be done to overcome the problems associated with the Teacher Appraisal scheme of the 1980s and 1990s. The teacher appraisal process largely declined in the 1990s because the teaching profession saw it as being time-consuming, bureaucratic, mechanistic and threatening ('a scheme to weed out the incompetent teacher'). It failed to link with teacher effectiveness in the classroom and personal development. These perceptions are not easily overcome, without proper investment in communication and training programmes.

I believe that performance management can deliver significant benefits to both individuals and schools. There is a potential win/win situation here. In recent Hay surveys of headteachers and teachers we found evidence of more positive attitudes towards performance management. We need to build upon these attitudes to give practical support to schools. It is critical that all staff, particularly team leaders, are engaged in the preparation for the performance management process. It is important that schools are allowed to implement the performance management process without other initiatives being 'dumped' upon them. There is a real danger of initiative overload in schools. The performance management process presents a real opportunity to create significant change within schools: change both in the way managers in schools define and measure 'performance', and in the way they manage staff and handle the performance management process. Performance management is a powerful change process and should be treated with due respect.

The 'new' performance management process must succeed where the old appraisal scheme failed. It will do so if it focuses on teaching and classroom practice, if it is not perceived as threatening, if it reinforces collaborative behaviour in schools, and if it enables the sharing of good practice and professional dialogues within schools. Also it is essential that the 'new' performance management should be forward-looking. It must not reflect the old 'deficit model' of performance management; it must encourage and reward those skills and behaviours which enable teachers and schools to be successful in the knowledge society. Schools must be not only places of learning but learning organisations, where personal development and improvement are embedded in the culture.

We have designed this book to be a series of practical guides for the headteacher, team leaders, teachers and support staff. There is little on theory; much on the practical. For those schools that genuinely want to develop their performance management process towards world-class 'leading edge' practice, this book will be invaluable.

We have set out our picture of a performance management process that is appropriate for the forward-looking teaching profession, in which we emphasise the importance of self-management, continuing professional development and self-directed change.

We are planning to supplement this book with a series of one-day conferences in order to explain our concepts and run some of the practical sessions. We hope to see you there!

Franklin Hartle

Background

There are still many organisations that do not have a formal process for managing performance. Yet all organisations – schools included – manage performance.

> How else do you ensure quality, know what your priorities are and, more basically, know what your job is involves?

The key to successful introduction of performance management lies in the acceptance by all staff that it is a core management process designed to support smarter ways of everyday working: a common sense and valuable way of doing things. All schools in England are now in the process of implementing performance management, with varying degrees of enthusiasm and from a variety of different starting points.

In implementing performance management, it is very easy to let the procedures, the forms and the timetable take over, and to lose sight of why you are implementing the process. In our experience, the most effective performance management process is that which supports the way you work and manage, not gets in the way. This leads to improved motivation and performance rather than simply establishing a whole new burden of bureaucracy.

> The best systems are those that support the way you work and manage.

To this end, we have designed this guide to be practical, and included user-friendly exercises and checklists. Sections 1, 2 and 3 outline the key issues which need to be addressed when implementing performance management. Sections 4 and 5 operationalise these issues into a series of practical steps for team leaders and teachers. The final Section 6 outlines ways in which the performance management process can be monitored and evaluated.

1

Designing and implementing performance management

This section has been written for those of you involved in designing and implementing the performance management process. It will help you to:

- understand the principles and benefits of performance management;
- design and implement a 'fit for purpose' process for your school.

WHAT IS PERFORMANCE MANAGEMENT?

There is no standard definition. Here are a few to think about:

- a process that links teachers, support staff and their respective roles to the success of pupils and the school;
- a process for establishing a shared understanding of what has to be achieved and how, and of managing staff in such a way that it will be achieved;
- a process for ensuring that staff are doing the right things in the most effective way to the best of their ability.

WHY ARE WE DOING THIS?

The short answer is because the government has told you to, but that might be taking a somewhat narrow view.

Ask yourself and your colleagues this question:

What does performance management mean to you? (Answer in one word or phrase.)

Among the words and phrases you may find:

Appraisal	Getting clarity	Stressful
Objectives	Feedback	Divisive
Time-consuming	Recognition	Team working
Bureaucratic	Development	Rating
Planning	Merit pay	Progress

The emphasis should be on management and motivation. This does not conflict with performance measurement. It will enable you to get more from your efforts to implement performance management. Getting staff motivated by, and through, performance management is the key challenge.

WHAT'S IN IT FOR YOU? (WIFY?)

Implementing performance management should deliver:

- greater clarity of roles, objectives and behaviours;
- more active management of performance by everyone in your school;
- more focused training and development;
- smarter ways of working;
- recognition of good performance;
- addressing of poor performance.

BELIEFS THAT UNDERPIN SUCCESSFUL PERFORMANCE MANAGEMENT

- Staff are committed to doing their best to contribute to the success of the school.
- The best person to be responsible for the quality of his/her work is the person doing the work.
- The success of the school depends upon its ability to unlock the potential for growth and development in the staff.
- People work more effectively when they are clear about what they have to do, and why, and get feedback and recognition for what they have contributed through their job.

PRINCIPLES OF OUR APPROACH

The performance management process will fulfil its potential if it is developed into a process that gets at the heart of what motivates staff at work. Ideally it will:

- provide maximum opportunity for staff to manage their own performance;
- be linked to continuing professional development;
- be 'fit for purpose': in other words it will fit, or represent, how you want the school to operate in terms of values and beliefs.

Team leaders will provide direction. The team leader's role is to challenge and support the team and to ensure the performance management approach is applied consistently to high quality standards.

Effective performance management is about changing ways, attitudes and behaviours, resulting in:

- improved self-esteem through recognition of contributions and achievements;
- improved staff capability through continuous learning and development;
- a better quality of teaching through setting objectives which require things to be done differently, and better and ongoing feedback/discussion about classroom practice;
- better teaching through clarifying roles and priorities and setting high professional standards for all staff.

MAKING IT WORK IN YOUR SCHOOL

- Focus on management processes that build a motivating climate, and emphasise supportive management skills and a continuous process of review.
- Use flexible, frequently-updated planning and regular feedback. Promote self-management and development.
- Recognise and reward good performance.
- Over time, aim to reduce the reliance on forms and procedures.

Table 1.1   Action/monitoring list

Action required	To be completed by	Resources/details/notes	Actual date completed
Design 1. Staff consulted on the flexible aspects of policy. 2. Policy agreed with governing body. 3. System designed (flow diagram). 4. Timetable agreed. 5. Pro formas selected/ designed. 6. Process for monitoring and evaluating the PM system in place.			
Perceptions 7. Staff aware of the purpose of PM, main stages and their own role. 8. Staff survey forms completed.			
Capability 9. Team leaders appointed. 10. Review officer appointed. 11. All staff provided with skills and knowledge to engage in the system. 12. Team leaders trained in skills required to review performance and write review statements.			
Implementation 13. Stage 1 reviews take place; objectives set. 14. Objectives and individual plans completed. 15. Copies received by headteacher.			

Action required	To be completed by	Resources/details/notes	Actual date completed
16. Lesson observations completed.			
17. Copies received by headteacher.			
18. Lesson observations completed.			
19. Final reviews completed.			
20. Copies of review statements received by headteacher.			
21. System evaluated.			
22. System improved as a result of evaluation.			
23. Report sent to governing body.			

Getting started

In our experience there are three key elements to the successful design and implementation of performance management. In many ways, designing the process is the easy bit. Successful implementation will arise only if perceptions of staff are addressed and individual capabilities are developed. It is the attention paid to perception and capability that really makes the difference.

In the sections that follow we will give some guidance on developing all three areas.

You may find the 'action list' in Table 1.1 helpful in reviewing your progress.

DESIGN ISSUES TO ADDRESS

Your core process

The core performance management cycle is a simple one – plan, monitor/coach and review.

The cycle reflects what effective teaching is all about. Plan the

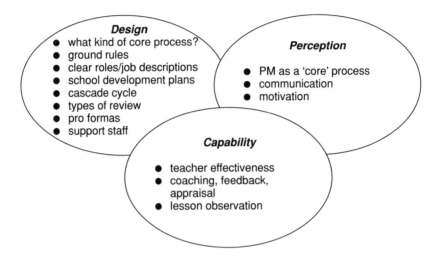

Figure 1.1   Implementing performance management: the three key elements

Figure 1.2   Design issues to address

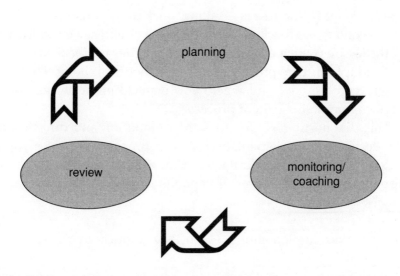

Figure 1.3   The core performance management cycle

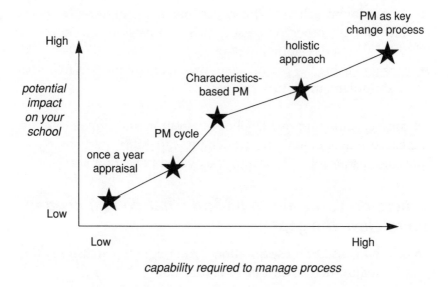

Figure 1.4   Where are you now?

lesson, manage the lesson – taking stock at various times, giving and receiving feedback to and from pupils – and review at the end of the lesson (which enables you to plan better for the next).

To adapt this core process to fit your school, it is helpful to know where you are now and where you want to get to in terms of a performance management process.

This diagnostic tool provides the foundation and direction for the design and implementation of your process. It enables you to judge what kind of performance management process/es will be appropriate and the level of capability required to manage the process.

- Are you implementing (or using) a **once-a-year appraisal** system?
- Are you implementing (using) a basic **performance management cycle** like the one shown in Figure 1.3, that is, planning, monitoring, and reviewing?
- Are you using the professional **characteristics** as an integral part of your system?
- Is your approach to performance management **holistic**, that is, linked with other processes such as Investors in People, or your school development plan?
- Are you using the performance management process to initiate and implement **culture change**?

Of course, achieving this level of integration and impact requires increased management and leadership capability, particularly for the team-leader role. This aspect is covered in Section 3.

Where do you want to be and what do you need to do to close the gap?

To help you answer these questions, you might like to use a simple questionnaire such as the one in Figure 1.5.

Rate the current PM process (0–10) [ ]

Score index: 1 = strongly disagree, 4 = strongly agree

		Score			
	Attitudes	1	2	3	4
1.	We have clear reasons for having performance management (PM)				
2.	Our team leaders are strongly committed to PM				
3.	Team leaders understand and work well with PM				
4.	This school has a clear sense of direction and purpose				
5.	Staff in this school are in no doubt that performance is what matters				
6.	We have a clear idea of what support PM requires and who should provide it				
	Skills				
1.	Individuals are clear about what is expected of them in their jobs				
2.	My team leader and I agree on our priorities				
3.	We are used to setting goals for ourselves				
4.	Team leaders motivate staff to develop and achieve their goals				
5.	Timely and effective feedback/support is given and received				
6.	We have a development programme to improve performance management skills				
	Process				
1.	The school development planning process provides a clear focus for our activities				
2.	School priorities are well communicated through the school				
3.	Monitoring standards of performance is a regular management activity				
4.	The current PM process helps to improve performance				
5.	Performance judgements are fair and consistent				
6.	The current link between pay and performance is fair				
	Total score				

Instructions for the diagnostic questionnaire
Decide on who to consult and ask each of them to complete the questionnaire.
Add up the scores for attitudes, skills and processes and produce a total score (maximum 72).
If you score below 36, you have a large number of issues that need addressing. The scores of individual items can give you some help with priorities.
A score of 36–54 suggests that there are some issues that need addressing.
If you score over 54, you have a solid platform for introducing performance management or developing your process further. You probably only need to take action if you have any individual items which score only 1 or 2.
This is a very effective tool to use with different departments for comparison purposes. It is not a full diagnostic and should not be used as a full audit of your performance management process.

Figure 1.5   A simple diagnostic questionnaire

ESTABLISHING THE GROUND RULES

One of the key elements in the implementation stage is to establish the ground rules by which you will operate the performance management process within your school. The process ought to 'live and breathe' the values which underpin how you relate to each other as a school community. Some of the areas that you will need to clarify are:

- confidentiality rules;
- resourcing (particularly time for lesson observation, review meetings, objective setting);
- lesson observation protocols;
- team leaders' training (now and in future);
- measuring performance of pupils and using the data;
- link with pay (particularly post-threshold);
- appeals machinery;
- audit of performance management process;
- reconciling different approaches to performance management from professional associations;
- role clarity (for key roles for performance management process – eg team leader, job holder).

CLEAR ROLES/JOB DESCRIPTIONS

The basic performance management cycle can be developed to incorporate individual role profile information and other information, setting the performance in context such as school objectives and (if appropriate) team objectives, as shown in Figure 1.6.

A starting point for any management of performance must be clarity about roles. (See the role profile in Figure 1.7.)

Using this information you will have a common understanding within the school on what is needed from those playing individual roles to meet the school's overall objectives.

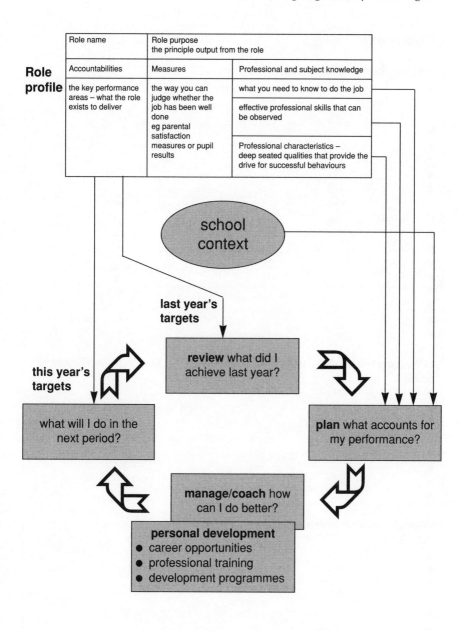

Figure 1.6 Developing the performance management cycle

Role profile

What are the key accountabilities for the role?
-
-
-
-
-
-
-
-

How is success measured?
-
-
-
-
-
-
-
-

What professional skills and knowledge are required to deliver the account-abilities?
-
-
-
-
-
-
-
-

What professional characteristics are required?
(see Section 3)
-
-
-
-
-
-
-
-

Figure 1.7   Role profile

SCHOOL DEVELOPMENT PLANS

A key aspect of performance management is the alignment of individual objectives with departmental and whole-school objectives. This means that there will be an end benefit both for the individual and for the school.

For staff to be able to work towards win/win objectives they need to understand what are the key objectives of the school. School development plans are generally too complex and mainly consist of maintenance and action plans. Often the targets for improvement are lost amongst all this.

One way forward is to produce the **4 to 6 key priorities of the**

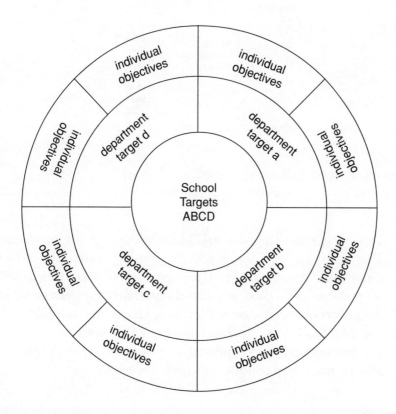

Figure 1.8   Aligning school-team – individual objectives

school (preferably on no more that one side of A4). Staff can use this when preparing their draft objectives as part of their self-review.

A STEPPED CASCADE CYCLE

There is merit in considering a stepped cascade to your performance management planning cycle, as shown in Figure 1.9.

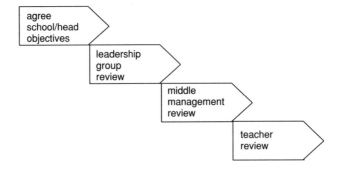

Figure 1.9   A stepped cascade cycle

1.   The headteacher agrees his/her objectives with governors. This assumes that there will be enough external advisers trained and available. If not, and you do not want this to hold up your process, then you could agree draft objectives which the governors review once they have an external adviser.
2.   The headteacher conducts leadership group reviews.
3.   The leadership group conducts middle-manager reviews.
4.   Middle managers conduct teachers' reviews.

Timing

How often will you go through this cycle?

- Annually?
- Twice a year?
- Quarterly?

There is no rule about frequency. Do whatever suits your school best.

Remember that while people are getting used to it, a new performance management process can feel like an extra burden (eg completing forms and preparation), so make sure you allow time for it to be done effectively.

As pupil progress is the focus of performance management, most schools will eventually choose the first half of the Autumn term for reviews and/or planning to take place.
The advantages of this are:

- Examination data are available.
- The school should have set its priorities and objectives for the school year.
- Teachers know which classes they are teaching and can therefore set targets appropriately.

Objectives can be set in a longer time-frame than one year, but team leaders should ensure that 'milestones' are set indicating what progress is expected at shorter time intervals.

ESTABLISHING THE PUPIL-PROGRESS FOCUS

Threshold assessment has made a big impact in terms of making staff analyse and use pupil-progress data. We therefore suggest that you use a similar format for performance management: only this time the process is not retrospective.

The key aim is to get staff to monitor the progress of their pupils and to use the resulting data to set a pupil-progress objective and then to review it.

Staff use a pro forma in three stages, as shown in Table 1.2.

Table 1.2 Three stages in the use of a pro forma

Step 1 (early Sept) • context; • prior attainment; • expected attainment	Completed with the help of the team leader or line manager. This is important as staff may either over or under-estimate the expected attainment. Also staff may be guided by commercially or school-produced predicted performance data, and this may have to be modified, taking into consideration the context of the class. It is therefore best achieved in discussion with the team leader or line manager.
Step 2 (Sept/Oct) • set pupil progress objective	Teachers set a draft objective prior to their review, with reference to the school improvement plan and departmental improvement plan. This is discussed with the team leader and a final pupil progress objective agreed.
Step 3 (following July or Sept) • final attainment • evaluation	Completed in discussion with either team leader or line manager. The evaluation takes into consideration pupil movement in and out of the class and any factors outside the teacher's control. It is the evaluation rather than the final attainment that is used as a basis for the final review.

The advantages of this process are:

■ Individual teachers are made responsible for monitoring their pupils' progress – an extension of their mark books.
■ The pupil-progress objective is selected with reference to the school improvement plan and in the context of all classes taught.
■ The final review process can take into consideration the progress of all pupils – not just those in the class or cohort selected for a pupil-progress objective.

TYPES OF REVIEW

A self-review based on threshold standards

Many of your staff have already invested a large amount of time in a self-review against threshold standards. In a few years' time more of your staff will be doing the same. It therefore makes sense to base a professional standards framework on the threshold standards.

As many of your staff hold posts of responsibility, we have included an additional set of standards for leadership and management. (See the professional standards framework pages in Section 5.) This professional standards framework can be used at the end of the cycle as a frame of reference against which team leaders can make a professional judgement about the overall performance of the teacher.

A 360-degree review

Self-review is very powerful. Genuine and meaningful improvement really comes about only when the teachers themselves decide that they need to learn and they need to improve an aspect of their teaching.

However, a self-review is conducted from a first-person perspective and therefore may not represent a true picture of the situation. Staff may wish to use the standards framework to elicit feedback from a different perspective, for example from pupils or colleagues. This can initially be made an optional part of your system although we think it is essential.

Team objectives

Some schools are considering the use of team objectives, especially for the leadership group. Their argument is that team members should all have the same pupil-progress objective, and all either meet or not meet the objective.

Identical objectives can be agreed, but it may be helpful to discuss and agree as a team who has 'prime' responsibility for the delivery of each objective. The rest of the team will then have a 'shared', contributory or remote responsibility for delivery. This method of agreeing team objectives has the added advantage of identifying those objectives with little or no driving force, and those where everyone is 'having a go', and you may be getting duplication of effort, as shown in Figure 1.10.

Objectives area	Fred	Jo	Chris	John	Jane
strategy	P	R	S	S	C
leadership	R	S	P	S	C
operations	S	P			S
development		S	P	S	
etc...					

P = prime S = shared C = contributory R = remote
NB To improve clarity, only one person should be 'prime' for each objective.

Figure 1.10   Team planning matrix

Individual improvement plans will be different. Each individual plan will describe what each member of the team will need to do in order to help meet the common objective.

DECIDING ON PRO FORMAS

Pro formas are an invaluable way of tracking and recording. However, they are not the reason we implement a performance management process! They are a means to an end. If they do not have a clear and definite purpose and value, they can be viewed as a total waste of time.

Table 1.3 lists the pro formas included in this book (see also Sections 4 and 5).

Table 1.3   Pro formas included in this book

Name	Description
1. Self-review	This allows teachers to record their strengths and areas for improvement following a review against a professional framework based on threshold standards. As a result teachers can formulate draft objectives.
2. Recording objectives and improvement plan	An alternative pro forma that considers learning and development as a means to achieving objectives rather than an objective in its own right.
3. INSET application/ tracking/ evaluation	A multi-puprose form that can be used as an application for learning and development, for planning and evaluation of learning and development, and as a learning log to be kept by teachers in their professional development portfolio. Designed to provide a strong evidence base for IIP (Investors in People).
4. Monitoring pupil progress	An extension of the teacher's mark book that emphasises the teachers' accountability for the progress made by the students they teach.
5. Lesson feedback	A form which allows the 80:20 rule and allows for 80% confirmation of good practice and 20% focus on how things could be better next time.
6. Final review of performance	A more structured form than that produced by the DfEE, allowing for comments under threshold headings as well as recording progress against objectives.

The DfEE has provided some sample forms with the performance management framework. We suggest that you choose (and adapt) the forms that best meet your needs as a school.

INCLUDING SUPPORT STAFF

The inclusion of support staff is optional. Investors in People schools already include support staff in a developmental review process, and you will want to continue in the same vein. Support staff can use performance management to improve their performance and professional development. We suggest this process:

1. Make a commitment to include all support staff in performance management. Discuss with support staff how you see the process helping them improve their performance, and what the benefits are to them.
2. Agree a process. Discuss with support staff how the process for teachers will be adapted to meet their needs. Build this into your performance management policy.
3. Establish who will be team leader for whom. This may involve teaching staff acting as team leaders for some staff (eg technicians), while other staff may have the school bursar as team leader. Where there are groups of staff working only a few hours, such as midday assistants, consider the merits of a team review.
4. Agree a timetable and select the pro formas to be used. Try to use the same pro formas where possible and amend where necessary. The following pro formas can probably be used with little amendment:
    – objective-setting and improvement plan pro forma.
    – the DfEE final review statement pro forma.
5. Provide training for individuals and team leaders. Team leaders may require training to set objectives, monitoring and feedback skills and assessment and reporting skills.
6. Follow the performance management cycle, as reiterated in Table 1.4.

Table 1.4   The performance management cycle

Planning	Monitoring	Review
<ul><li>review job description</li><li>agree objectives and record improvement plan</li><li>agree how observation or monitoring will take place and when</li><li>confirm review dates.</li></ul>	<ul><li>may include observation if appropriate</li><li>or talking to people who receive the service from the individual.</li></ul>	<ul><li>team leaders make a professional judgement and write a brief statement summarising the overall performance of the individual.</li></ul>

2

Addressing perceptions: bringing your staff on board

THE PERCEPTION OF PM AS A CORE PROCESS

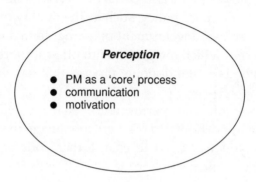

Figure 2.1   Perception

We firmly believe that performance management is a core process in the school. One of the key first steps that you have to take in communicating the performance management process is to convince your staff of its benefits to them. You must be able to answer their question, 'What's in it for me?'

Sometimes it might be appropriate, and more impactful, to invite your staff to identify the potential benefits. That approach is likely to generate more commitment from the staff.

An early meeting with staff on the development of performance management should cover the following issues:

■ What's in it for me? (WIFM?)
■ The skills that team leaders will need to have.
■ Staff fears/concerns/issues.
■ What do we care about in this school: that is, what are our values about how we relate to others?

■ What can we build upon (for example, Investors in People)?

■ What do we want performance management to be like in our school?

Ideally you should link discussions on performance management to other areas of school policy, such as the quality of teaching and learning, and school development planning, so that it is positioned as a core process which integrates with other important aspects of school life, not as a 'stand-alone' process that has little impact on school life.

If you position the performance management process as providing an opportunity to teachers to manage their own performance, then you will need to ensure that your process actually reflects this. This means providing all staff with:

■ **training and development opportunities;**

■ a **professional standards framework** against which to self-review;

■ a whole-school system of **recording pupil progress data,** together with training to enable the staff to access and use the data;

■ **team leaders trained** and competent in coaching and monitoring techniques;

■ **encouragement** to set draft objectives, having completed a self-review ahead of the first objective-setting meeting;

■ **regular feedback** on their performance and recognition of achievements;

COMMUNICATION

Getting the buy-in and commitment of the staff to performance management will be critical to ensuring its success, for them, for the school and for the pupils.

Regular and positive communication will help develop commitment. You can consider communications in two stages:

1. **Information**: to provide clarity, raise awareness and develop understanding of the performance management process.
2. **Involvement**: to generate acceptance and build commitment.

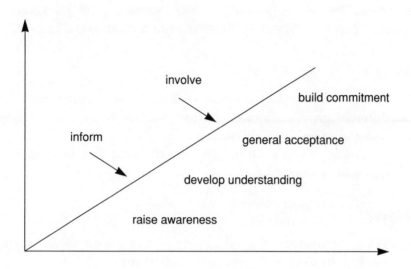

Figure 2.2   The two stages of communication

The fundamental purpose of communication in an organisation is to enable and energise employees to carry out its strategic intent.

The best communications are:

- fit for purpose;
- timely;
- clear (avoid jargon and keep it short and simple);
- consistent (what you say and what you do);
- coherent;
- sincere;
- genuine;
- two-way.

A COMMUNICATIONS CHECKLIST

Who?

■ Who do you want/need to communicate with?

■ What are their current issues? Messages or information matched to real issues will have more relevance and impact.

What?

■ What are your key messages? These may be different for different groups. Try not to communicate more than three or four messages at one time.

■ It's not what you want to tell them, it's what they want to hear that will have impact.

How?

■ What are your usual ways to communicate with staff? Do you need to do something different to create impact?

■ The more sensitive the issue (the more anxiety it could potentially raise), the more important it will be to have face-to-face communication

Bear in mind that staff briefings and presentations (even with questions and answers) can often feel 'one-way' and are not very involving. If you can manage it, a facilitated discussion is much more involving.

When?

■ When will people be most receptive?

ESTABLISHING THE RIGHT ATMOSPHERE

Performance management means challenging staff in a safe and supportive environment. You need staff to set challenging objectives which may help them to improve their performance.

This means doing things differently and better. It means taking risks!

To encourage staff to take risks there has to be a 'safety net', an environment in which it is all right to make mistakes – although it is not all right to make the same mistake twice!

You need to build in credit for progress made, even when this falls short of the objective, when staff have made a serious attempt to change their practice and improve their performance.

People tend to feel less threatened and defensive when:

- they are given the space and opportunity to work things out for themselves;
- they have a sense of safety, are relaxed, and have trust and confidence in the person listening to them;
- they have a sense that they are appreciated as human beings and as professionals, and are able to think, decide, act and feel naturally.

MOTIVATION

Managing performance effectively involves managing and influencing motivation.

Research has shown that individuals' performances are an outcome of both their ability and their motivation. Often the implementation of performance management concentrates on developing ability through development planning, and motivation through incentives (pay bonuses and so on). Unfortunately, this is to miss the opportunity to consider the wider aspects of motivation.

What is motivation?

The concept of motivation is that there are driving forces within all of us which we use to achieve goals, in order to fulfil personal needs and expectations.

The carrot and stick approach

One of the simplest motivation theories is that of the carrot and stick. Imagine you have an immobile donkey. One way to get it to move is by beating it with a stick, the other is to entice it with a carrot. From your point of view it doesn't matter which approach works as long as one does.

This simile illustrates some of the most deeply (even if not consciously) held beliefs about motivating others, that it is necessary to provide a reward or threaten a punishment. However, individuals are qualitatively different from donkeys, so there must be a more sophisticated way!

The carrot or the stick must be applied constantly if it is to continue having an effect. It is an external stimulus. It is only when a person wants to do something of his or her own volition that we can see genuine motivation.

MANAGING MOTIVATION IN THE PERFORMANCE MANAGEMENT CYCLE

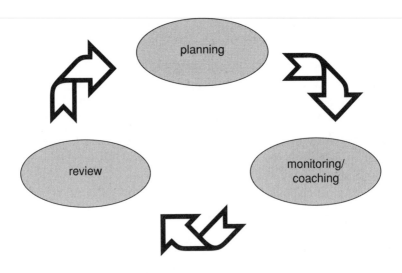

Figure 2.3   Motivation in the PM cycle

Stage 1: Planning

This stage embraces:

- definition of job responsibilities;
- setting performance expectations;
- objective-setting for the beginning of the period.

To maximise motivation at this stage, the objectives set should be clear, specific, challenging and accepted by the individual. This is achieved through the individual's involvement in the objective-setting process.

If there is resistance to accepting objectives, participation in objective-setting may improve 'ownership'.

In addition, an individual's expectations must be managed in terms of rewards. What is expected of the person in terms of skills/behaviours, and how their skills/behaviours link to rewards, must be communicated effectively.

Stage 2: Monitoring/coaching

This stage embraces:

- monitoring;
- feedback and coaching;
- development.

Feedback and coaching will act as reinforcers and shapers to previous behaviour.

Care must be taken, as it should not be assumed that all types of feedback motivate and improve performance. For feedback to be motivating, it must be timely, accurate, from a credible source and constructive.

Stage 3: Reviewing

This stage embraces:

- formal performance review.

Reinforcement and equity are extremely important at this stage. Consequently, recognising appropriate behaviours and rewarding them in appropriate ways is paramount.

Inequities in recognition can result in either improved or reduced performance, owing to changed motivation levels. Hence, it is important that experience, ability and effort should justify differences in pay and responsibility.

The problem which always arises at this stage is that one person's equity is another's inequity. This highlights the importance of determining the expectations of the individual at the beginning of the performance management process, in the planning stage.

3

Developing
capability

TEACHER EFFECTIVENESS

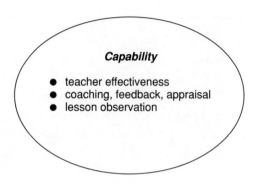

Capability

- teacher effectiveness
- coaching, feedback, appraisal
- lesson observation

Figure 3.1   Developing capability

In 1999/2000, HayGroup carried out major research for the DfEE into teacher effectiveness (DfEE 2000b). This section looks at the principles identified in that research and how they can be applied in performance management.

WHAT MAKES A GOOD TEACHER?

Ask yourself, what were the characteristics of the best teacher I ever had?

Teachers who really enjoy their work are constantly looking for ways to be more effective. At the same time, the government wants to reward excellence in classroom teaching, to keep more high-quality professionals in the classroom rather than moving into school management.

The HayGroup research for the DfEE provides a clear picture of what excellence in classroom teaching looks like. It can help teachers to plan their professional and career development.

The HayGroup research identified three main factors within teachers' control that significantly influence pupil progress:

■ teaching skills;
■ professional characteristics;
■ classroom climate.

Each provides distinctive and complementary ways in which teachers can understand the contribution they make. Each should be incorporated in your performance management process. None can be relied on alone to deliver value-added teaching.

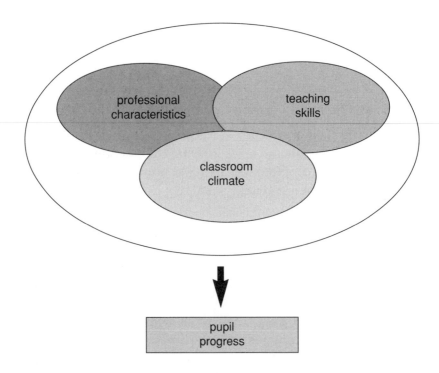

Figure 3.2   The model of teacher effectiveness

The three factors are different in nature. Two of them – professional characteristics and teaching skills – are factors that relate to what a teacher brings to the job.

The **professional characteristics** are the ongoing patterns of behaviour that combine to drive the things we typically do.

The **teaching skills** are those 'micro-behaviours' that the effective teacher displays in the classroom.

While teaching skills can be learned, sustaining these behaviours over the course of a career will depend on the deeper-seated nature of professional characteristics.

Classroom climate, on the other hand, is an output measure. It allows teachers to understand how the pupils in their class feel about the dimensions of classroom climate that influence their motivation to learn.

All competent teachers know their subjects. They know the appropriate teaching methods for their subjects and curriculum areas, and the ways pupils learn. More effective teachers make the most of their professional knowledge in two linked ways.

One is the extent to which they deploy appropriate teaching skills consistently and effectively in the course of all their lessons: the sorts of teaching strategies and techniques that can be observed when they are at work in the classroom, and which underpin the national numeracy and literacy strategies.

The other is the range and intensity of the professional characteristics they exhibit inside and outside of the classroom: ongoing patterns of behaviour which make them effective.

Pupil progress results from the successful application of subject knowledge and subject-teaching methods, using a combination of appropriate teaching skills and professional characteristics. Professional characteristics can be assessed, and teaching skills can be observed.

Classroom climate provides another tool for measuring the impact created by a combination of the teacher's skills, knowledge and professional characteristics.

Taken in combination, these three factors provide valuable tools for a teacher to enhance the progress of his/her pupils.

TEACHING SKILLS

Teaching skills are 'micro-behaviours' that the effective teacher constantly exhibits when teaching a class. They include behaviours like:

- involving all pupils in the lesson;
- using differentiation appropriately to challenge all pupils in the class;
- using a variety of activities or learning methods;
- applying teaching methods appropriate to the national curriculum objectives;
- using a variety of questioning techniques to probe pupils' knowledge and understanding.

In the HayGroup report they are clustered under the seven Ofsted inspection headings for ease of use. (See Figure 3.3.)

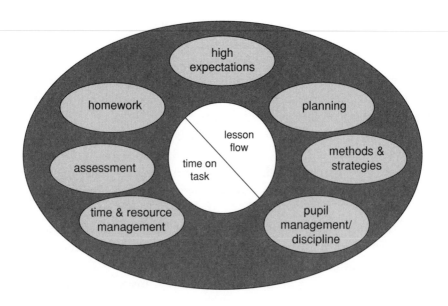

Figure 3.3   Teaching skills: the key areas

The effective teacher:

- has high expectations for pupils and communicates them;
- uses a structured and planned approach for all lessons and units of work;
- employs flexible teaching strategies;
- has a clear strategy for pupil management;
- manages time and resources wisely;
- uses a range of assessment techniques.

PROFESSIONAL CHARACTERISTICS

Professional characteristics are deep-seated patterns of behaviour which outstanding teachers display more often, in more circumstances and to a greater degree of intensity than do less effective colleagues.

They are how the teacher does the job, and have to do with self-image and values; traits, or the way the teacher habitually approaches situations; and, at the deepest level, the motivation that drives performance.

Sixteen characteristics contribute to effective teaching. (See Figure 3.4.) This does not mean that all effective teachers demonstrate strength in all sixteen characteristics. Strength in each of the five clusters is required. Certain different combinations of characteristics within these clusters can be equally effective.

This is not a static, 'one size fits all' picture. Effective teachers show distinctive combinations of characteristics that create success for their pupils.

CLASSROOM CLIMATE

Classroom climate is defined as the collective perceptions by pupils of what it feels like to be a pupil in any particular teacher's classroom, where those perceptions influence pupils' motivation to learn and perform to the best of their ability.

Each climate dimension represents an aspect of how the pupils feel in that classroom. They are defined as follows:

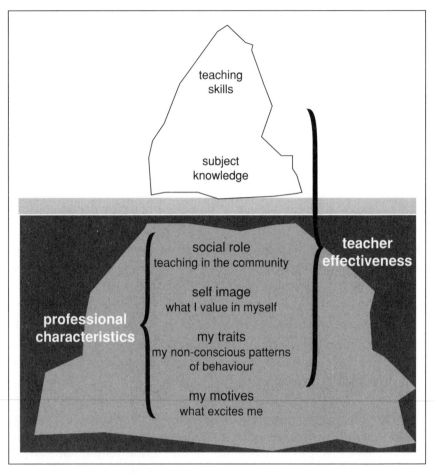

Figure 3.4   The iceberg model

- Clarity around the purpose of each lesson. How each lesson relates to the broader subject, as well as clarity regarding the aims and objectives of the school.
- Order within the classroom, where discipline, order and civilised behaviour are maintained.
- A clear set of standards as to how pupils should behave and what each pupil should do and try to achieve, with a clear focus on higher rather than minimum standards.
- Fairness: the degree to which there is an absence of favouritism, and a consistent link between rewards in the classroom and actual performance.

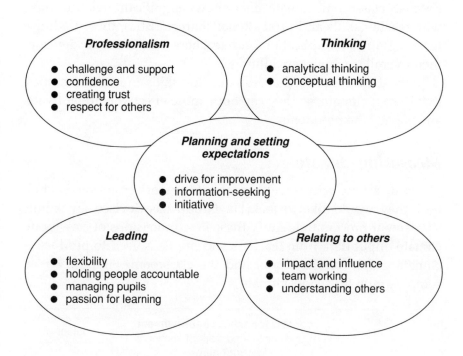

Figure 3.5   The model of professional characteristics

- ■ Participation: the opportunity for pupils to participate actively in the class by discussion, questioning, giving out materials, and other similar activities.
- ■ Support: feeling emotionally supported in the classroom, so that pupils are willing to try new things and learn from mistakes.
- ■ Safety: the degree to which the classroom is a safe place, where pupils are not at risk from emotional or physical bullying, or other fear-arousing factors.
- ■ Interest: the feeling that the classroom is an interesting and exciting place to be, where pupils feel stimulated to learn.
- ■ Environment: the feeling that the classroom is a comfortable, well-organised, clean and attractive physical environment.

Because classroom climate also shows significant relationships with teacher skills and professional characteristics, these findings have significant implications for teachers who wish to develop their overall teaching capability.

To the degree that teachers can develop skills and characteristics that impact climate, so they can hope more effectively to motivate and engage their students.

Measuring climate

The issue is how people feel now about the work environment and how they would like to feel. HayGroup has devised an online assessment process to identify these key dimensions of classroom climate. Input data from teachers and pupils is used to produce a climate graph for the school and the classroom. Figure 3.6 is a sample graph for school climate.

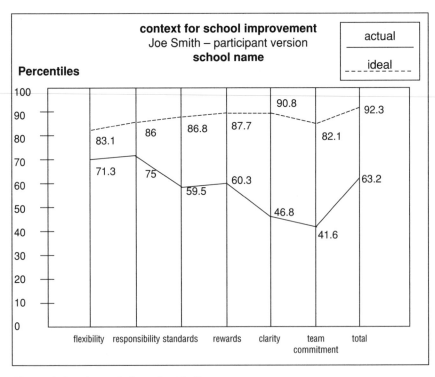

Figure 3.6   A graph for school climate

Does it work?

Our research in schools clearly indicates that a high climate leads to high performance. We found a strong correlation between measurements of school climate and levels of school performance (rated by Ofsted inspectors). (See Figure 3.7.)

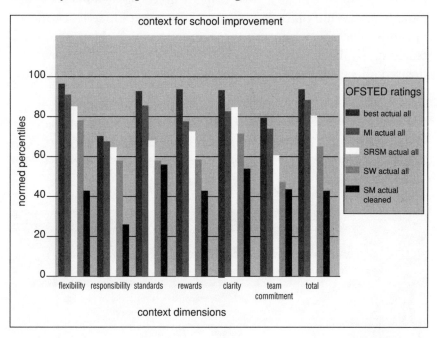

Figure 3.7   Correlation between school climate and school performance

Our research with teachers found that both primary and secondary schoolteachers were able only partially to predict their students' assessments of the climates within their classrooms. This suggests that, by administering the classroom climate question-naire to a sample of their pupils, teachers could gain greater insight into their pupils' perception of the climate within their classrooms. This would enable them to focus their effective teaching skills and characteristics on those aspects of the climate that should be improved, and, where necessary, help them under-stand better what aspects of their current teaching practices need to be developed.

Furthermore, waiting to see whether or not a teacher is capable of motivating pupils to perform, by measuring students' accomplishments at the end of the year, is a cumbersome and unwieldy way for teachers to discover whether or not their efforts to improve their teaching practices are bearing fruit. The online measurement of whether any of the desired changes in classroom climate are taking place offers a much more rapid feedback mechanism to teachers, regarding the degree to which changes in their teaching skills and professional characteristics are having the desired effects.

Upward feedback from pupils

School and classroom climate questionnaires are available via the Internet from www.transforminglearning.co.uk. Figures 3.8, 3.9 and 3.10 illustrate what you will find there.

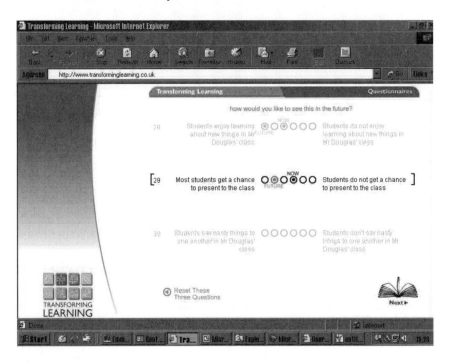

Figure 3.8   Sample of the online climate questionnaire

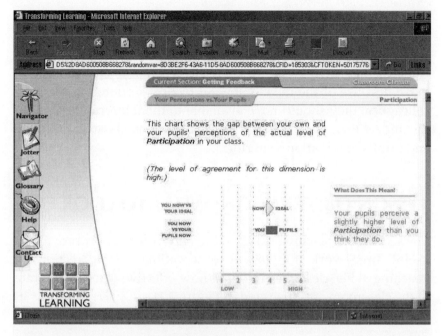

Figure 3.9   Sample of online feedback

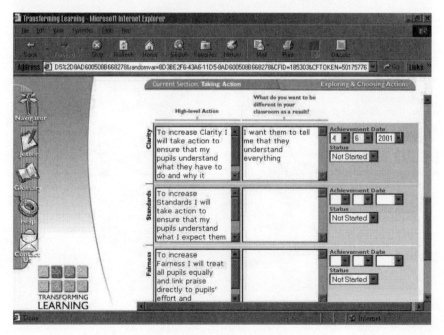

Figure 3.10   Sample of the online action planner

Despite the demonstrated impact of classroom climate on pupil motivation and performance, it is rare for British teachers, or teachers in other countries, to receive structured feedback on the climates they help create in their classrooms. If teachers are to make best use of the developmental feedback offered to them by colleagues, they should have available to them information about the impact their current behaviour is having on classroom climate and pupils' motivation to perform.

LESSON OBSERVATION: WHAT TO LOOK FOR

The section on 'teaching skills' in the HayGroup report provides a useful framework for lesson observations. Each section of 'teaching skills' describes in detail how effective teachers operate in the classroom, as illustrated in Figure 3.11.

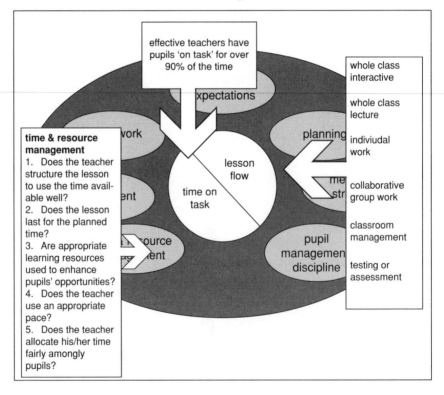

effective teachers have pupils 'on task' for over 90% of the time

whole class interactive

whole class lecture

xpectations

planning individual work

time & resource management
1. Does the teacher structure the lesson to use the time available well?
2. Does the lesson last for the planned time?
3. Are appropriate learning resources used to enhance pupils' opportunities?
4. Does the teacher use an appropriate pace?
5. Does the teacher allocate his/her time fairly amongly pupils?

lesson flow

time on task

collaborative group work

classroom management

pupil management discipline

testing or assessment

Figure 3.11　How effective teachers operate in the classroom

OBSERVING ONE ANOTHER

It is imperative to have a protocol for observing one another in the classroom. Here is a set of principles:

- Agree why you are doing it, and what you intend to get out of the process.
- Look for specific evidence, or examples of events that you can discuss together.
- Concentrate on building strengths, not on dealing with weaknesses.
- Always look for what you can learn as well as what you can teach others.
- Invite others into *your* classroom.

4

A guide for team leaders

This section supports you, as a team leader, in helping others improve their performance through the performance management process.

The skills and approaches illustrate the day-to-day practice of leaders and managers who understand that the continuing success of their team and school depends upon their continuing professional development.

THE TEAM LEADER AND PERFORMANCE MANAGEMENT

Performance management should be a process of continuous improvement and learning. It is about improving pupil performance through improving teacher performance. Team leaders are expected to:

- help teachers to identify objectives and create an improvement plan;
- challenge and support teachers, and ensure alignment of personal objectives with department and school targets/priorities;
- provide guidance, coaching and support to help others improve their performance;
- provide regular, timely and constructive feedback;
- make objective judgements about performance.

Key factors in determining the success of performance management are:

- the skills and commitment of the team leader;
- the degree to which a teacher is empowered to manage his/her own performance;
- the quality of the relationship established between the team leader and the teacher.

The key to being a successful team leader is:

■ enabling teachers to solve their own problems with support from the team leader;

■ constant focus on raising the self-esteem and capability of the teacher.

SETTING OBJECTIVES

The objectives you set with individuals in your team will work best if they are:

■ directly related to their aspirations;
■ directly related to the team's/department's/school's priorities.

We recommend that you hold a discussion to set objectives with each member of your team. Following the five key steps shown in Figure 4.2 will help you. These steps are explained in order below.

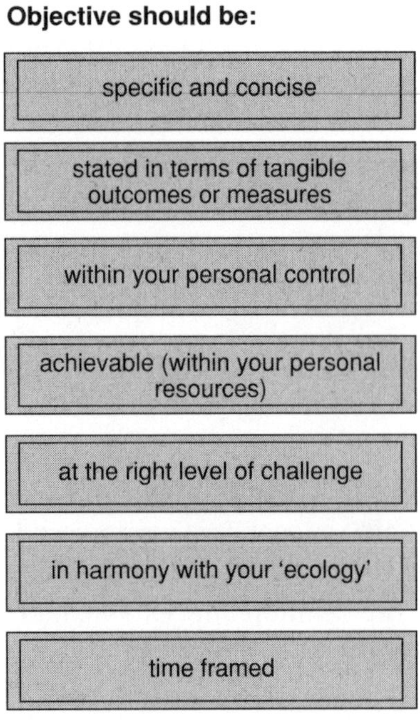

Objective should be:

specific and concise

stated in terms of tangible outcomes or measures

within your personal control

achievable (within your personal resources)

at the right level of challenge

in harmony with your 'ecology'

time framed

Figure 4.1   What makes a quality objective

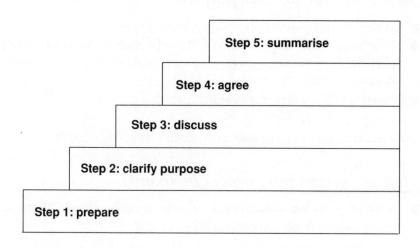

Figure 4.2   The five key steps in setting objectives

Step 1: Preparation

- Before planning the discussion, reflect on the individual's role and try to see the role through his/her eyes.
- Review the school's priorities, departmental objectives and own performance plan.
- Sketch out some tentative objectives in anticipation of what may be developed formally with the individual.
- Schedule the meeting in a private and comfortable location and allow enough time for open and honest discussion. If the individual feels rushed or that you are not concentrating on the discussion, he/she is less likely to attach importance to the process and might feel less committed.
- Ask the individual to prepare the draft objectives from his/her perspective before the meeting. Provide appropriate information (such as pupil progress data and school/departmental improvement plans) ahead of time to assist him/her in preparing this draft.

Step 2: Set the agenda/purpose

- Welcome the individual and put them at ease.
- Emphasise the importance of this discussion to continuous performance improvement and personal/professional development.
- Outline the agenda, for example:
  - agree objectives;
  - summarise the discussion and offer ongoing support.

Step 3: Discuss job purpose/demands

- Referring to job description or role profile, ensure there is clarity around job purpose and demands.

Step 4: Agree 'objectives' and 'needs'

- Discuss the school's priorities and/or team leader's objectives with the individual.
- Review the individual's proposed objectives.
- Jointly agree between three and six objectives.
- Jointly agree an action plan.

Step 5: Summarise/agree support required

- Ask for questions/concerns.
- Write up the results of the meeting.
- Encourage the individual to come to you at any time to discuss problems.
- Express confidence in the individual's ability to achieve the objectives.

HELPING TEACHERS TO SET OBJECTIVES

It is your responsibility to ensure that the objectives agreed are aligned to those of the school and team. In addition the objectives should:

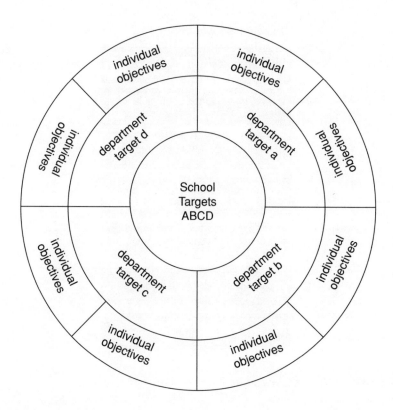

Figure 4.3   Setting school–team–individual objectives

■ Be win/win objectives. This means benefit for the teacher and benefit for the school or team. This can be achieved by aiming to set objectives where the circles in Figure 4.3 overlap.
■ Include one pupil-progress objective. Where the teacher has a management or leadership role, there should also be a second pupil-progress objective that relates to progress across a subject or year group.

The DfEE use the term 'professional development objectives'. Professional development is a means to an objective rather than an objective itself. The DfEE give the following example of a professional development objective:

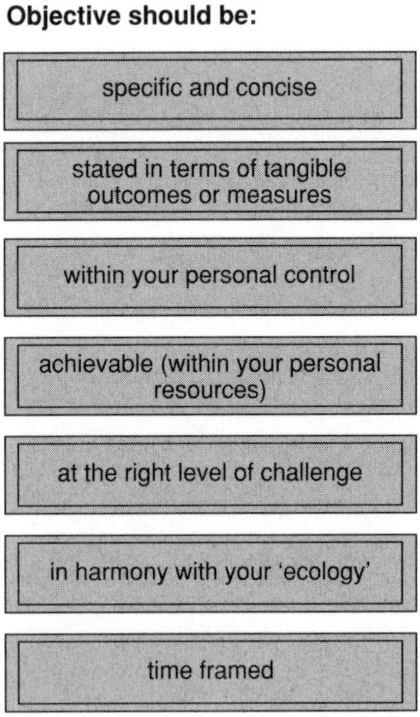

Objective should be:

specific and concise

stated in terms of tangible outcomes or measures

within your personal control

achievable (within your personal resources)

at the right level of challenge

in harmony with your 'ecology'

time framed

Figure 4.4   What makes a quality objective?

To develop expertise in the teaching of drama with the aim of directing a school production within two years.

When the objective is to 'direct a school production in two years', developing expertise in the teaching of drama is part of what the teacher needs to do in order to achieve this objective. This learning and development of expertise is therefore listed in the improvement plan.

Remember: objectives are flexible. If factors change and the objectives set are no longer appropriate, then they should be amended or re-set. The performance management process should 'live' during the year. It should not be a once-a-year meeting.

REACHING CONSENSUS

If the individual's draft objectives do not meet the accepted criteria, you may have to probe and explain to reach a consensus.

If the individual proposes an objective that is set too low:

- Discuss it, in order to discover why it is too low.
- Identify obstacles that the individual feels will interfere with achieving better performance or meeting a higher standard.
- Work with the individual to overcome these obstacles (for example, by reference to professional characteristics and/or teaching skills).
- If appropriate, highlight additional resources or extra assistance that will enable the individual to set and achieve a more challenging objective.
- After discussing the resources needed to overcome the obstacle, reconsider whether the objective is, in fact, too easy to achieve: that is, too much into the 'comfort zone'.

If the individual proposes an objective which is unrealistically high:

- Ask him/her to explain the plan in detail.
- Ask why the individual thinks he/she can achieve the objective (especially if it is in a new area, or in an area where he/she has previously been unsuccessful).
- Discover whether any estimates or resource requirements are overly optimistic.
- Look for unrealistic assumptions about the availability of supplies, equipment, support services and people (including cooperation needed from others).
- Based on the discussion, reconsider whether the objective is actually too stretching. If so, mutually agree on a more realistic objective. Remember to let the individual know that you appreciate his/her willingness to attempt a difficult objective, but that it is important to set challenging but realistic objectives.

What if we still cannot agree?

One of the reasons you cannot agree may be that your mode of behaviour and the mode of behaviour of the teacher are in conflict. Your behaviour and the behaviour of the teacher need to be purposeful. (See the description of purposeful behaviour below.)

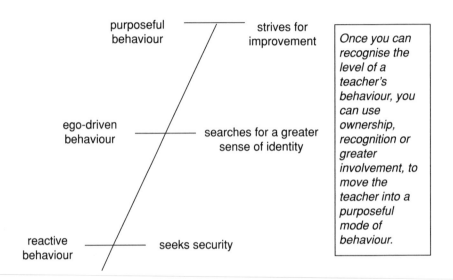

Figure 4.5   Types of behaviour

Reactive behaviour is determined by the environment and is defensive in its nature. It has a past focus ('It never used to be like this', 'Appraisal never worked') and is centred around a desire to survive.

Teachers exhibiting reactive behaviour have a basic need for security. They focus on rights, and strive to acquire more rights to provide a sense of progression and a route to 'ownership'. The more rights they have, the more secure they feel.

Ego-driven behaviour is determined by self. It has a present focus, and can be offensive.

Teachers exhibiting ego-driven behaviour have a need to be

recognised and to establish their identity. They search for ways of getting involved in projects which provide interaction with others. The greater the involvement and interaction, the greater their sense of being able to influence others.

Purposeful behaviour has a future focus and is characterised by versatility.

Teachers exhibiting purposeful behaviour seek personal development which benefits themselves and the school. They seek to increase their capacity and strive for increasingly high standards. Their end goal is personal improvement.

Where there is still disagreement

If the individual disagrees with an objective that you may suggest as a team leader, and if it is important for accomplishing school objectives:

■ Restate your understanding of the individual's perception of the situation.
■ Show empathy and state that you need his/her acceptance of the objective you proposed in order to meet the needs of the department and school.
■ Discuss the need for more resources or support, if appropriate.
■ Remember that you have to agree with the teacher over the selection of the final objectives.

The regulations state that where agreement cannot be reached, then you should write out the objectives you have determined, and the teacher should sign to say that he/she does not agree, and why. Should you reach this stage, it is probably better to seek help from senior managers who may be able to help reconcile the situation.

USING PROFESSIONAL CHARACTERISTICS IN FEEDBACK SESSIONS

As a reminder, professional characteristics were discussed in Section 3. They:

- are underlying characteristics that enable someone to perform a job better in more situations, more often, with better results;
- are those factors that distinguish the best from the rest in a given role;
- can be deep-seated qualities (motivation traits and so on), or easily-observed skills or knowledge;
- can be measured;
- are not the tasks of the job, but are what enable people to do the tasks.

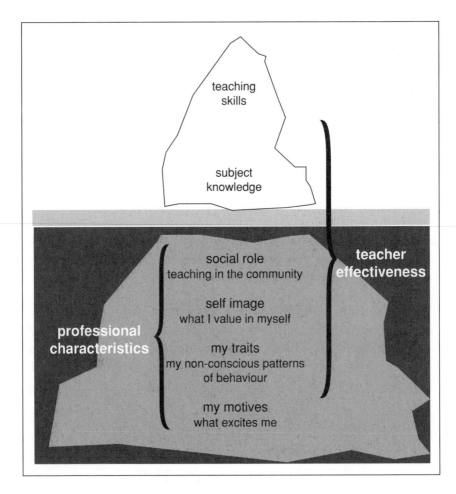

Figure 4.6   The iceberg model

Section 3 talks about the characteristics of an effective teacher. These 'characteristics' should be used in your performance management discussions. They identify the 'how' of effective teaching. They will give you a framework for identifying gaps in individual performance and suggesting development actions.

We suggest that you identify together the three or four key characteristics that will make most difference to the performance of the teacher concerned. Trying to talk about all of their characteristics at once will be confusing.

MONITORING AND COACHING PERFORMANCE

Key to the success of performance management is the continuous process of monitoring and coaching including:

- lesson observation;
- providing support;
- coaching.

Lesson observation

In Section 3 we looked at the use of lesson observations. It is an important way for a teacher to get feedback from others, so again we are referring to it briefly here. Also in Section 3, there are references to teaching skills, which provide a framework for lesson observation, and some key questions to ask in each skill area.

Know what you want as outcomes before you start any observation. Your plans and actions should be focused on achieving your outcomes, for example:

- Objective information regarding the performance of the teacher.
- The teacher to feel good about the aspects of his/her lesson which are noteworthy.
- The teacher to improve one or two areas of his/her teaching.

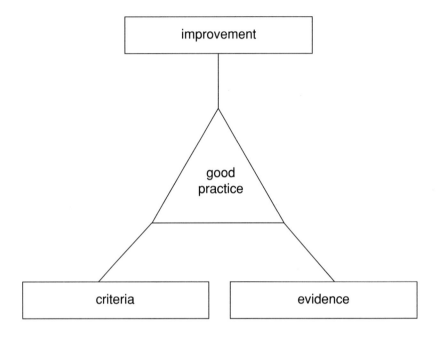

Figure 4.7   A framework for lesson observation

You will need to meet the teacher ahead of any observation to agree what the focus of the lesson will be and to agree 'ground rules':

■ By the end of the lesson you should be able to identify areas of good practice and areas for improvement.
■ This is done by comparing written, spoken and observational evidence against clear and agreed criteria.
■ You may be looking at effective teaching or just one particular aspect which may relate the teacher's objectives.

Table 4.1   Lesson observation: good practice points

Before the lesson	During the lesson	After the lesson
Agree practicalities ● Which lesson, when, where? ● Will there be a focus? ● What will you tell the pupils? ● Where will you sit? ● Will you get involved in the lesson? ● What if a pupil misbehaves? *View the lesson in context* ● Where does this fit in the scheme? ● What happened before/what comes next? ● Discuss the nature and context of the lesson. ● What are the learning outcomes? *Agree on feedback* ● As soon as possible aftewards. ● If not possible, then a brief verbal summary followed by a formal feedback session. ● Written feedback to be provided.	● Arrive before the start of the lesson. ● Use shorthand to record specific examples of what happened in the lesson that meets or does not meet the standards in the school's criteria. ● Talk to pupils, but only when this can be done without interrupting the lesson. ● Look at mark books and pupil books. ● If the unexpected happens and the lesson is a disaster and beyond the control of the teacher, leave and arrange another time to observe. ● Thank the teacher at the end of the lesson.	Try using the 'six pack' model: 1. Introduction. Set the scene and purpose of the feedback (this is an opportunity to put on your team leader hat: your teacher may also be a close friend). 2. Ask the teacher to describe the elements of the lesson that he/she felt went particularly well, giving specific examples. 3. Add the aspects of the lesson that you felt went well, with specific examples. 4. Ask the teacher to describe how, if he/she were to teach the lesson again, he/she would do things differently, and why. 5. Add suggestions (if appropriate) of how the lesson could be improved if it were to be taught again. 6. Summarise the feedback and any actions for improvement and support and how these will be monitored. Finish on a positive note.

PROVIDING EFFECTIVE FEEDBACK

Know what you want as an outcome

If you want the teacher to feel good about aspects of his/her performance, and determined to improve one or two aspects of his/her teaching, then you need to provide feedback in a way which is likely to achieve this outcome. The following strategies will help.

Reduce the amount of negative feedback

Aim for an 80:20 ratio of positive to negative feedback. If there are several areas of concern, then prioritise and focus on how one or two areas can be improved.

If you focus on too many negative aspects, the teachers are likely to become defensive, blame the pupils, parents, lack of resources and so on. Once this happens, teachers are unlikely to put improvements in place, because they have just convinced themselves that their unsatisfactory performance has been caused by factors out of their control.

Focus on the teacher's needs, not yours

Instead of '*I* was really pleased with the way pupils summarised their understanding at the end of the lesson', try '*You* should be really pleased with...'. After all, the point of the lesson is not to please you, or to have the lesson delivered to your liking. If things go well, then you should encourage the teacher to feel good about it. Again, when providing advice, say 'If *you* want less interruptions to the lesson, try...' (again focusing on his/her needs).

Separate the person from the practice

It is *their* practice that is outstanding, or *their* practice that needs improving.

Be specific

Avoid general comments such as 'The lesson got off to a good start.' Rather, be specific and say, 'That cartoon on the OHP really caught the attention of the class.' If you did feel that things were excellent or poor, describe what happened in the class that led you to those conclusions.

> The more specific the feedback, the greater the scope for learning, development and improved performance.

The detailed descriptions of teaching skills and professional characteristics in the HayGroup model of teacher effectiveness enable you to be very specific when giving feedback to colleagues.

Be objective

Be descriptive rather than evaluative. Inform the teacher of the effect his/her actions had on you or on the pupils. So rather than 'Your instructions for the practical activity were very unclear', say, 'When I asked several of the pupils, they said they were confused and unsure as to what they needed to do to carry out the practical.'

Focus feedback towards the future

The teacher cannot do anything about lessons already taught: they are in the past. He or she can do things differently and better in the future, so talk about what the teacher can do to make his/her teaching better next time. This converts negative feedback to positive feedback.

Use 'and' rather than 'but'

You will be amazed at how much more positive a sentence sounds when the word 'but' is removed: for example, in 'Your lesson was very practical but excluded some pupils.'

Leave them with a choice

Offer information about the teacher's performance in a way that leaves him or her with a choice about what to act on and what not. You may examine the consequences of any decisions, but you do not prescribe change – this needs to be the individual's decision.

END-OF-YEAR REVIEWS

You may have conducted informal reviews of progress as part of your monitoring and coaching throughout the year, but it is likely that your formal review will be one year after the initial objective-setting. It may be combined with agreement of objectives for the next year.

As with the planning discussion, you and the teacher should both prepare your own views on performance in advance. If performance has been managed continuously throughout the year, there should be no surprises.

Preparation

Figure 4.8   End-of-year reviews

- Review objectives and professional characteristics/skills developed over the year.
- Be clear about your and the individual's objectives for the review meeting.
- Agree an agenda.
- Coach the individual so he/she feels more comfortable contributing.
- Take a provisional view of actual performance.
- Note any specific feedback to be given.
- Spend time thinking about how he/she will feel and react.
- Make sure that time, timing and venue are appropriate and organised.

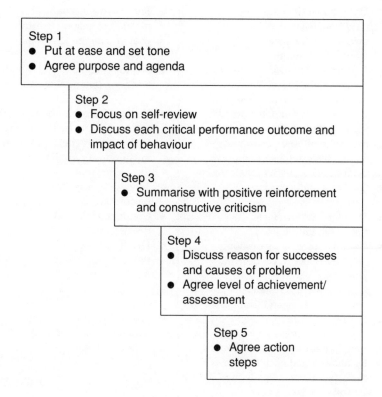

Figure 4.9   The performance review meeting

Dos and don'ts of performance reviews

Table 4.2 illustrates dos and don'ts in preparing for and conducting a review. Managers often feel uncomfortable about conducting this discussion. It is useful to review this list of reminders to help guarantee a successful experience.

Table 4.2   Dos and don'ts of performance reviews

Do	Don't
● Gather performance data from a variety of sources for the full year. You will need the teacher's permission to gather data from colleagues.	● Focus on recent performance data only.
● Use managerial judgement based on behavioural evidence to balance the overall assessment.	● Try to use a mechanical formula or rate each critical goal or competency in the same way.
● Emphasise the description of results against objectives and demonstration of behaviours.	● Be judgemental or focus on the teacher's potential worth.
● Explain how you determined the assessment. Give specific examples of how performance results were achieved and how behaviours were demonstrated.	● Discuss the performance of other teachers, compare the teacher with other teachers, or be vague, mysterious or apologetic about the assessment.
● Confront and correct poor performance.	● Tolerate unacceptable performance.
● Develop performance improvement plans.	● Conduct a one-way discussion.
● Conduct a two-way session; get the teacher's reaction and perceptions. Make it clear that you are interested in his/her feelings and thoughts.	● Dwell on past problems, blame the employee, or put him/her on the defensive.
● Focus on future improvements and development.	● Assume that performance enhancement is for poor performers only.
● Remember that each teacher is	
● Remember that each teacher is expected to enhance his/her performance each year.	
● Remember to discuss both strengths and development needs.	● Focus on weaknesses only.

MAKING A PROFESSIONAL JUDGEMENT

Use evidence from:

- monitoring pupil progress;
- lesson observations;
- the teacher's professional development portfolio (if he/she has one and is agreeable).

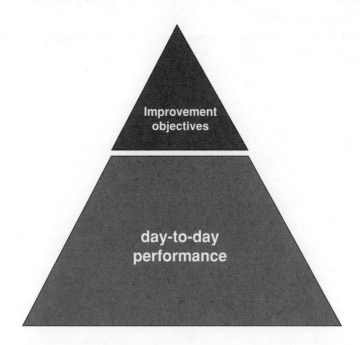

Figure 4.10   Making a professional judgement

Some hints on making a judgement:

- Your judgement needs to be in the context of the job and to take account of the teacher's career stage.

- Any judgement should be based on the degree of improvement achieved by the teacher, rather than whether the objective has been met. In other words, focus on what is now better and different, and the degree of 'added value' which has resulted.
- You may wish to comment on the actual progress against expectations of all pupils taught. If you and the teacher have monitored pupil progress using the recommended pro forma, you will be able to use this.
- Reference day-to-day performance against a professional standards framework.
- Draw upon all available evidence, including that provided by the teacher.

5

A guide for
teachers

As a teacher, performance management offers you the opportunity to take an active part in your future development through self-review and self-management. This section shows you some ways in which you can take an empowered approach to managing your own performance.

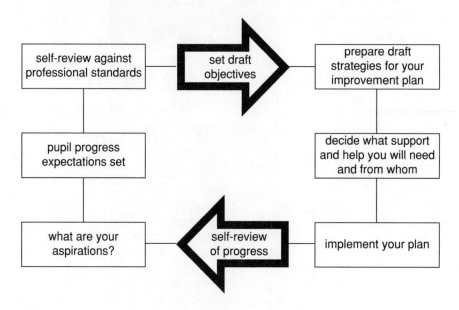

Figure 5.1   Key steps in managing your own performance

SETTING YOUR OBJECTIVES

There has been much research on the importance of setting clear objectives for achieving success. Knowing what you want to achieve focuses your attention and brings to your notice things that might help you.

Objectives that are vague, almost wishful thinking, are unlikely to help you. 'I ought to lose some weight' rarely produces the desired result!

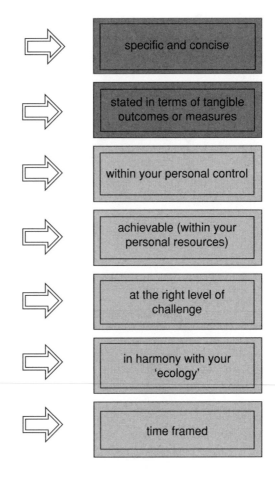

Figure 5.2 What makes a quality objective?

WHAT MAKES A QUALITY OBJECTIVE?

Objectives should be flexible. If factors change and the objectives set are no longer appropriate, then they should be amended or re-set. We suggest you do this with your team leader to avoid confusion later.

Overall performance will be higher as a result of setting challenging objectives, even if the objectives are not quite met.

If you have a management responsibility, such as leadership group or head of department or subject coordinator, we suggest you set two pupil-progress objectives:

- an individual objective for a cohort of pupils you teach;
- a management objective for whole year/whole school.

Examples of objectives

Individual pupil progress objective
To reduce the number of predicted U grades for year 11 science class from 12 to between 4 and 8 by the end of the year.

Management objective for head of year
To improve the attendance of year pupils from 87 per cent to 93 per cent by the end of December

TRACKING PUPIL PERFORMANCE

Using the pro forma shown as Figure 5.3, and following the three key steps listed in Table 5.1, can help you to keep track of progress.

Table 5.1   Tracking pupil performance

Step	Action	Comments
Step 1 (Preferably early September)	Context. Prior attainment. Expected attainment.	Complete this section for each class with the help of your team leader or line manager. You may be guided by commercially or school-produced predicted performance data. This may have to be modified to take into consideration the context of the class.

Table 5.1 *continued*

Step	Action	Comments
Step 2 (Just before, and during, your review meeting)	Set a draft pupil progress objective. Agree a pupil progress objective.	With reference to the school improvement plan and departmental improvement plan, set a draft objective for one of your classes. To formulate this objective, you need to increase the expected attainment to add strength and challenge. The draft objective is discussed with your team leader and a final pupil progress objective agreed.
Step 3 (Just before your final review)	Complete final attainment and evaluation columns.	Again, this is completed in discussion with your team leader or line manager. The evaluation takes into consideration pupil movement in and out of the class and any factors outside the teacher's control. It is the evaluation rather than the final attainment that is used as a basis for the final review.

Figure 5.3   A format for monitoring pupil progress/setting pupil progress objectives

Class/example With details of the class context (ability/absence rate/other factors)				
Prior attainment				
Expected progress				
Actual progress made				
Evaluation of progress				

SELF-REVIEW

Identifying your aspirations

Visualising

Self-review starts with knowing what you want for yourself.

A newspaper survey in September 1999 indicated that 45 per cent of those interviewed wanted to change jobs. The date was significant. Most readers had spent a summer vacation where they were able to 'switch off' and think about what was important to them and what they really wanted for themselves.

> Once you know what you want for yourself and where you want to go, then you can start making it happen.

If you don't know where you are going, then any road will do!

Successful objective setting results from using both parts of the brain, as in Figure 5.4.

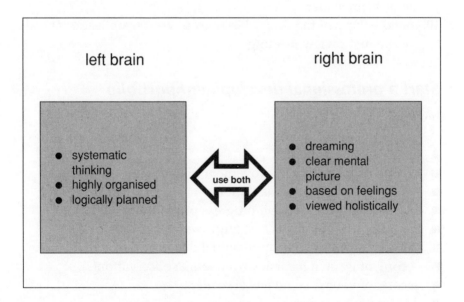

Figure 5.4   Using both sides of the brain

TEN STEPS FOR SELF-REVIEW

1. Know what you want for yourself – your aspirations.
2. Complete step 1 of the pupil-monitoring pro forma (with the help of your team leader/line manager).
3. Set a draft pupil-progress objective.
4. Complete the self-review pro forma using the professional standards model.
5. Ask colleagues/students to review your performance.
6. List strengths and possible areas for improvement.
7. Prioritise areas for improvement with reference to the draft pupil-progress objective and school and departmental improvement plans.
8. Write draft objectives for these prioritised improvement areas.
9. Think about what you will do differently to achieve these objectives, what resources and professional development you may require and what support and help you require from your team leader.
10. Send a copy of the draft objectives to your team leader ahead of the first review meeting.

Start a professional development portfolio

Include:

- your job description;
- a copy of the school improvement plan;
- your self-review documentation;
- your monitoring of pupil progress pro forma;
- your copy of objectives and improvement plan;
- a log / record of your professional development activities;
- a copy of written feedback from lesson observation(s);
- a copy of your final review statement;
- letters from parents, photographs, certificates;
- anything else you want (it is yours!).

Use it to:

- assemble evidence to help complete a threshold application;
- write a letter of application for a new job;
- influence your team leader in writing your final review statement.

Threshold standard areas	Strengths	Areas for improvement
professional knowledge		
teaching and assessment		
professional effectiveness		
leadership and management		
professional characteristics		

Draft objectives (between 4 and 6 including your pupil progress objective)

-
-
-
-
-

Send your draft objectives to your team leader ahead of your review meeting to help frame your discussion.

Figure 5.5   Self-review summary

SEEKING AND RESPONDING TO FEEDBACK

You may seek feedback as part of your self-review. You will receive feedback as part of the lesson observation schedule. Regular feedback is vital in helping us improve our performance. It provides us with information from different perspectives. You may find the following advice helpful.

Listen to the feedback

Try not to reject or argue with it immediately.

This sometimes means listening to things that we would rather not hear. However if we are defensive or resistant, people may not provide feedback in the future – much to our disadvantage.

Listen carefully and ask for clarification if there is anything you are unsure of. Show encouragement – the person providing feedback may be nervous!

Be clear about what is being said and why

Avoid jumping to conclusions and becoming defensive.

Make sure you understand before you respond. Paraphrasing is a useful technique to check that you have understood what is being said.

Check it out with others rather than relying on one source

People view situations from different perspectives. Eliciting information from a variety of colleagues or sources (pupils, for instance) helps to provide a balanced view.

Ask for the feedback you want but may not get

If feedback does not occur naturally, you may need to ask for it. Sometimes feedback is restricted to one area of our practice, and we may need to request feedback on other areas which we would find useful.

Decide what you will do as a result of the feedback

The feedback will confirm where your practice is good and meets the standards and expectations of the school. It will also highlight areas where practice could be better.

Thank the person for giving the feedback

Constructive feedback is invaluable, and the least we can do is to thank the person for his/her help. In addition we could say which aspects of the feedback we have found useful.

SOME FREQUENTLY-ASKED QUESTIONS ABOUT THE REVIEW PROCESS

Who knows what my objectives are?

Your objectives and improvement plan are recorded during your initial review meeting. You keep a copy of the plan and a copy is held by the headteacher. Your team leader has access to this document. In addition, the staff development coordinator will be informed of any learning and development needs.

What if my head of department is not my team leader? How can he/she support me without having access to my objectives and knowing what they are?

That's a good question. Maybe you should provide your head of department with a copy.

We work as a team. How can we support one another to achieve objectives if we do not know what each other's objectives are?

Why not tell each other?

Do we have to use external data to set pupil performance targets?

Schools can choose to use the data they find most reliable and helpful. Remember that using external data may help with providing evidence for threshold assessment in later years.

What if I don't like my team leader?

Headteachers are responsible for appointing team leaders. As the relationship between teacher and team leader is crucial, head-teachers should be sensitive and ensure that team leader allocation pays attention to this. Heads can consult but they have the final decision. All team leaders should be in a position to help and support teachers in the pursuit of their objectives.

I decided not to submit a threshold form. Can I opt out of performance management?

Everyone is to have a performance review every year, whether they want one or not. In almost all organisations improvement is expected – you can't opt out of improvement.

What if it all starts going wrong?

At the end of the cycle you can complain to the school's review officer, who is normally the headteacher. A review officer is appointed from the governing body to deal with complaints from teachers who are dissatisfied with their review, when the head is their team leader. Review officers can order final statements to be retained or ask for another review to take place.

Can I choose the lesson(s) that my team leader observes?

Schools will decide on how this is organised.

What is the link between performance reviews and pay?

This is three-step process:

1. Team leaders make a professional judgement about the overall performance of their teachers.
2. Heads consider this information, together with any other information they may hold, and make recommendations about pay to governors.
3. Governors make decisions about pay.

FINDING THE TIME

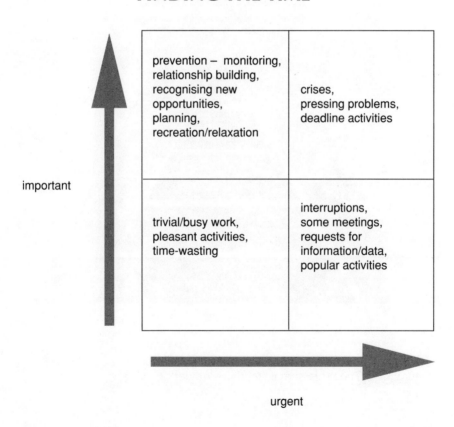

Figure 5.6   Time management

The reason we do not seem to be able to find time is that most of our main priorities tend to be in the important and urgent categories (see Figure 5.6). It is these activities that result in stress, burn-out and crisis. Performance management is an investment to reduce the number of future crises.

THE PROFESSIONAL STANDARDS MODEL

(This is based on threshold assessment.) The standards model refers to four dimensions of teacher capability. Each dimension contains clusters of standards under a descriptive heading. (See Figure 5.7.)

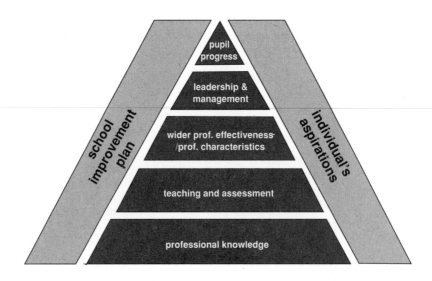

Figure 5.7   The professional standards model

For each cluster you can use the rating system:

M   Current level of performance is good and I need to MAINTAIN this level.
I   Performance in this area is reasonable with room for IMPROVEMENT.
C   My day-to-day practice does not reflect these standards and I need to CHANGE the way I am doing things.

As a result, you should be able to summarise your strengths and areas for improvement against each dimension. You can then prioritise these areas for improvement (through reference to school improvement plans) and set draft objectives for the prioritised areas.

Threshold applicants

If you have submitted a threshold application form, you have recently conducted a self-review, so, with reference to your form, list the areas you felt less confident about when filling in the form. In addition you may wish to review your performance against the leadership and management standards.

Table 5.2   Professional standards: knowledge and understanding

Description of good practice	M/I/C	Description of good practice	M/I/C
Up-to-date knowledge of techniques and practice 1. Incorporates cutting-edge aspects of subject taught into teaching and into the scheme of work, eg the use of fuel cells to power vehicles. 2. Draws upon accelerated learning techniques such as the use of mind maps and music to aid concentration and creativity. 3. Encourages students to visualise the outcomes of their work. 4. Learns new teaching techniques applicable to subject. 5. Engages in a subject-related discussion with colleagues, eg through a journal of a professional body. 6. Keeps up to date with developments in assessment methods. *Knowledge of subject* 1. Reads articles that contain up-to-date knowledge and information about specialist subject. 2. Incorporates new knowledge and understanding into scheme and lessons. 3. Uses students' everyday experiences to illustrate ideas and issues.		*Awareness and application of national strategies* 1. Incoporates ICT such as the use of DTP, word processing and spreadsheets into lessons and scheme of work. 2. Uses ICT to prepare lessons, maintain pupil records or to help improve progress through target setting. 3. Relates teaching to requirements for the curriculum as a whole, eg to develop information-seeking skills. 4. Enthuses students to consider careers in areas related to one's subject. 5. Includes aspects of key skills including literacy and numeracy into schemes and lessons where appropriate. *Post threshold standards for knowledge and understanding* 1. Continually maintains up-to-date knowledge of teaching techniques and evaluates their effectiveness in the classroom. 2. Researches an unfamiliar area of subject to prepare a new teaching approach to a topic for use by other teachers. 3. Regularly questions the ways things are taught	

Description of good practice	M/I/C	Description of good practice	M/I/C
4. Responds to students' questions with a range of examples drawn from subject knowledge. *Wider curriculum knowledge* 1. Takes opportunities for professional development to keep up to date on curriculum developments, eg effective formative assessment. 2. Refers to syllabuses/ programmes to study in other key stages when developing schemes of work. 3. Works with colleagues in primary schools, for example, to ease transition problems. 4. Relates subject to requirements in other subjects in the curriculum. Reads about initiatives such as Early Learning Goals, social inclusion measures for post-16 students, University for Industry.		and make suggestions for improvements. 4. Regularly, as a matter of routine, devises lessons, homework exercises and tests which are differentiated and incorporate correct knowledge at the appropriate level. 5. Devises novel learning activities that elicit good learning from pupils. 6. Identifies issues that lead to future curriculum developments in subject taught. 7. Deconstructs complex elements so that the underpinning ideas can be established and taught to a class, a group or an individual. 8. Uses a range of contexts drawn from global, national, local and personal contexts, to illustrate lessons and schemes. 9. Introduces a citizenship and PSE dimension to lessons and schemes 10. Focuses on creativity in teaching.	

Table 5.3   Professional standards: teaching and assessment

Description of good practice	*M/I/C*	*Description of good practice*	*M/I/C*
Planning effectively 1. Sets up sequences of lessons to address strengths or a particular weakness in learning in an individual, group or whole class. 2. Discusses planning with colleagues. 3. Reviews and improves scheme with colleagues, making appropriate improvements based on feedback. 4. Changes a lesson plan during the lesson in response to feedback from pupils. *Communicating objectives* 1. Draws pupils' attention to the learning objectives of a lesson. 2. Reviews lessons with pupils in terms of meeting objectives. 3. Develops beliefs in pupils about what they can achieve. 4. Encourages pupils to visualise the successful outcomes of their work. 5. Sets assessment exercises that give pupils information about the standards of work expected. 6. Provides pupils with an overview of lessons and modules.		*Applying for optimum teaching strategies* 1. Varies tasks and approaches to provide appropriate challenge to individuals and groups of pupils, eg time, format and language. 2. Boosts confidence in a class, group or an individual, eg by encouraging pupils to take a pride in their work or use of display. 3. Uses a variety of methods to create interest and engage pupils' minds, eg by using stories, anecdotes and humour. 4. Uses modelling to help pupils understand difficult concepts. 5. Relates work to the everyday experience of pupils. 6. Tries out novel approaches to learning. 7. Encourages pupils to apply learning to unfamiliar situations. *Classroom management/ support* 1. Sets clear expectations of learning behaviour. 2. Takes action when standards of behaviour and learning fall below expectations. 3. Is consistent in the recognition of good behaviour achievement.	

Description of good practice	M/I/C	Description of good practice	M/I/C
Maximising homework and opportunities for learning 1. Sets appropriate homework that links with previous or next lesson. 2. Plans for pupils to learn from libraries, Internet, visits to museums, field trips, industrial visits and other opportunities for learning outside the classroom. 3. Sets exercises that require learning resources to be used which are based in the home and community. 4. Uses homework to help pupils explore links across subjects.		4. Provides constructive, formative feedback to pupils. 5. Explains an idea in different ways to pupils to take account of various levels of understanding. *Maximising the use of resources* 1. Gathers resources from businesses, charities and public services for use in lessons. 2. Uses classroom space effectively. 3. Works with a learning support assistant to enhance the quality of learning including joint planning. 4. Shares the management of learning with pupils, eg through providing opportunities for pupils to make choices about how they learn. 5. Involves pupils in self and peer assessment.	

Table 5.4   Professional standards: teaching and assessment continued

Description of good practice	M/I/C	Description of good practice	M/I/C
Evaluating pupils' progress 1. Sets assessment exercises that give pupils information about the standards of work expected of them and their relationship to class targets. 2. Develops a feedback system for pupils, for example by describing the meaning of marking system. 3. Uses data from National Curriculum Assessments, CATs, YELLIS or ALIS to plan lessons and guide and challenge individual pupils.		*Post-threshold standards* 1. Builds an element of risk into lessons in order to evaluate new teaching approaches. 2. Helps pupils to make connections with learning in other subject areas. 3. Regularly uses time for reflection on learning in lessons. 4. Devises homework activities that are appropriate extensions to lesson activity, and places emphasis on pupils learning how to manage their learning. 5. Strikes a balance between the main elements of teaching, whole class discussion, whole class instruction, individual work, collaborative group work, class-management activities, testing and assessment, review of learning.	
Making best use of assessment 1. Reviews performance with individual pupils or groups of pupils, for example after a learning task. 2. Works with pupils to help them set individual goals and targets (long and short term). 3. Provides ongoing feedback to keep pupils informed about how well they are progressing and how to overcome any problems. 4. Monitors pupils as individuals and takes action, where appropriate, to prevent them		6. Amends plans in order to develop pace and uses unpredicted opportunities to respond to unexpected weaknesses. 7. Demonstrates heavy emphasis on listening and responding to pupils. 8. Refines and evaluates	

Description of good practice	M/I/C	Description of good practice	M/I/C
experiencing undue difficulty and losing confidence, or to increase the challenge of the work they are doing. *Reporting clearly* 1. Regularly provides constructive, formative feedback to pupils. 2. Marks work to keep pupils informed about how well they are progressing and how to overcome any problems. 3. Provides constructive, formative feedback to groups and whole classes. 4. Reviews the performance of a pupil or whole class with colleagues in school. 5. Takes action to alert a parent or a colleague about under-performance in an individual or group.		questioning techniques over a specific period of time. 9. Identifies lessons that provide opportunities for pupils to make connections with learning in other subject areas. 10. Reviews expectations of pupils on a regular basis and as a consequence may generally raise expectations of some pupils. 11. Reviews the learning from homework in class on a regular basis.	

Table 5.5   Professional standards: professional effectiveness (includes threshold and post threshold standards)

Description of good practice	M/I/C	Description of good practice	M/I/C
Self-development 1. Uses mistakes as a source of improvement. 2. Seeks opportunities to build knowledge in one's subject and class-related areas. 3. Actively seeks feedback (from colleagues and pupils) as a major source of learning and improvement. 4. Reflects on own performance as a means of self-improvement. 5. Seeks opportunities to gain skills and knowledge in areas that may be useful, although currently outside areas of responsibility. 6. Plans activities to improve capability at work (eg observation of, and dialogue with, others, joins working parties, seeks training programmes to develop new skills.) *Adaptability and flexibility* 1. Operates within the school's values and expectations of staff. 2. Adopts means of communication and interaction that suit different groups (staff, parents, and pupils). 3. Plans ways of doing things that take account of different environments		*Maintaining a professional focus* 1. Maintains a professional approach when unduly annoyed, disturbed or disrupted. 2. Maintains objectivity when interpreting information such as exam results and pupil records. 3. Keeps things in perspective even when tired and frustrated. 4. Remains calm in difficult situations. 5. Works diligently to meet deadlines. 6. Copes effectively with ambiguity. 7. Maintains effectiveness and commitment in face of disappointment. *Initiative and innovativeness* 1. Takes action before being asked. 2. Sees an opportunity and takes action where this is within his/her control. 3. Makes suggestions as to how to improve things within the school and/or department. 4. Takes action to remedy situations where necessary even if he/she has no direct personal responsibility. 5. Questions the way	

Description of good practice	M/I/C	Description of good practice	M/I/C
and cultures. 4. Adjusts ways of working to changes in the environment (new syllabus, different teaching approaches, etc). 5. Alters strategies and modifies own behaviour where plans are stalling or the expected response does not materialise. 6. Seeks and acknowledges the merits of differing viewpoints. 7. Modifies a strongly-held opinion in response to contrary evidence.		things are done and makes improvements. 6. Develops new approaches to improve or replace existing procedures. 7. Originates alternatives to conventional thinking. *Maintaining and improving standards* 1. Works to meet standards of excellence as set by the school. 2. Applies school systems and procedures consistently (eg discipline procedures). 3. Ensures that all work is completed to agreed standards, eg the completion of schemes of work. 4. Sets high personal standards as an example to other staff and pupils. 5. Finds ways of using time and resources more effectively. 6. Points out redundant or unnecessary steps in methods and procedures.	

Table 5.6   Professional standards: leadership and management

Description of good practice	M/I/C	Description of good practice	M/I/C
Strategic thinking 1. Links day-to-day activities with the long-term strategic plan for the school. 2. Considers whether short-term goals will meet long-term objectives. 3. Establishes a course of action to accomplish a long-term goal or vision. 4. Analyses trends to anticipate long-term problems and opportunities. 5. Considers how present policies, processes and methods might be affected by future developments. 6. Prepares and reviews contingency plans for problems and situations that might occur. 7. Re-thinks key processes, the better to meet long-term objectives. 8. Establishes long-term school or departmental goals or projects. 9. Shares with others own view of the desirable future state of the school/department. 10. Develops a 'business' strategy for the school department.		*Strategic influencing* 1. Identifies the different needs of key people and adjusts strategies to influence them. 2. Lobbies key people to get agreement. 3. Switches tactics in changing situations in order to convince others. 4. Works with informal and formal systems to influence situations. 5. Takes politics, relationships and hierarchies into account when deciding the best course of action to influence people. *Team building* 1. Shares ideas and asks others for ideas. 2. Asks for help in solving problems, and offers help without taking away responsibility. 3. Uses a variety of ways to recognise and reward performance. 4. Acts to develop an atmosphere of teamwork and cooperation. 5. Takes action to make people feel their work is important. 6. Takes action in the wider school on the department's behalf. 7. Keeps people informed of the 'big picture': what	

Description of good practice	M/I/C	Description of good practice	M/I/C
Relationship building 1. Is aware of the feelings and emotions of others. 2. Is sensitive to changes in other people's moods or temperament. 3. Sees things from others' viewpoints. 4. Appreciates diverse approaches to thinking. 5. Understands the unspoken meaning in a situation. 6. Reflects feelings and emotions through mirroring and matching words, body language and intonation. 7. Detects the concerns, interests or emotions that seem to lie behind what people say. 8. Consistently acts to maintain the self-esteem of colleagues.		is happening. *Developing others* 1. Consciously acts as a role model for others. 2. Expresses positive expectations of others – treats people as he/she wants them to be, rather than as he/she perceives them. 3. Is personally available to provide guidance and advice if required. 4. Takes time to listen to, and offer help on, others' work-related problems. 5. Provides regular and timely feedback to colleagues. 6. Identifies the developmental needs of people. 7. Looks for opportunities in allocating tasks to develop individuals. 8. Clearly hands over responsibility for tasks to team members. 9. Matches organisational needs with those of individuals.	

6

Monitoring the impact of performance management

A GUIDE TO MONITORING THE IMPACT

The potential benefits arising out of the performance management process will vary according to the scale and quality of the implementation programme. At the lower level, the intervention should improve team leader/job-holder skills in setting objectives, managing own and others' performance and reviewing performance. Improved skills and a better-managed process should result in a more positive school climate in all dimensions, as shown in Table 6.1.

Table 6.1   Dimensions of a more positive school climate

rewards	more frequent and positive recognition of good performance and addressing performance issues	*clarity*	clearer idea of 'big picture' and how job contributes to it
team spirit	more collegiate working; identifying dependencies; team spirit should rise	*flexibility*	removing some of the constraints on performance
responsibility	more delegation with increased accountability for results	*standards*	the setting of challenging/realistic goals and monitoring of standards achieved

Therefore it is appropriate to use a school climate survey in order to measure the impact of performance management over time. If you decide to go down this route it is advisable to carry out a climate survey at the beginning of the implementation programme and to repeat it every twelve to eighteen months.

At the high level interventions, the performance management process should, in addition, bring about changed behaviours (through the competency-based approach) and better linkages with other processes. The expected benefits for a full performance management intervention are shown in Figure 6.1.

For team leaders
- effective communication of school plans and priorities
- definition of areas/ opportunities for performance improvement
- development of job holder in current jobs and future jobs
- development of more effective two-way communication with job holders
- improved training and development
- increased staff motivation
- opportunity 'add value' as a manager

For job holders
- clear direction on accountabilities, responsibilities, competencies and the 'big picture'
- feedback on how performance is measured by the team leader and others
- knowing what performance measures apply to their job
- indication on how they can improve their performance
- assistance with improving their performance
- better communication with team leaders
- more relevant training and development
- ability to assess and manage own performance

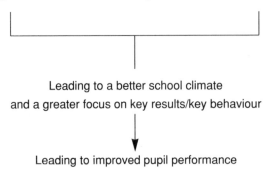

Leading to a better school climate
and a greater focus on key results/key behaviour

Leading to improved pupil performance

Figure 6.1   Expected benefits of performance management

MONITORING YOUR PERFORMANCE MANAGEMENT SYSTEM

■ Level 1 monitoring – did it happen? (use the 23 action point/monitoring list on page 6).
■ Level 2: monitoring the effectiveness of performance management in terms of outcomes.

The following questions are based on the evidence requirements for Investors in People. If the outcomes are positive then you have approximately two-thirds of the evidence required to be recognised as an Investor in People. You could ask a performance management consultant to carry out the survey.

Staff survey or interview of cross-section of staff

■ Do you believe the school is genuinely committed to supporting your development?
■ Give an example of how you have been encouraged to improve your own performance.
■ Give an example of how you have been encouraged to improve the performance of others.
■ Do you believe that your contribution to the school is recognised?
■ Describe how your contribution to the school is recognised.
■ How have you received appropriate and constructive feedback on a timely and regular basis?
■ Do you clearly understand what your development activities should achieve, both for you and for the school?
■ Explain how you have contributed to achieving the school's aims and objectives.
■ Do you understand what your team leader should be doing to support your development?
■ Describe how your team leader is effective in supporting your development.
■ Do you understand why you have undertaken development activities and what you are expected to do as a result?

- Give examples of what you have learnt (knowledge, skills and attitude) from development activities.
- Explain the impact of your development on your performance, the performance of your team and the school as a whole.

Additional questions for team leaders

- Does the school ensure that, as a team leader, you have the knowledge and skills you need to develop your staff?
- Do you understand what you need to do to support the development of staff?
- Give examples of actions that you have taken and are currently taking to support the development of your staff.
- Explain how, with your help, staff have improved the performance of the school, teams and individuals.

CREATING A BALANCED SCORECARD

Some schools are looking to use balanced scorecards as a way of tracking performance.

In your school's balanced scorecard the 'measures' you identify convey powerful messages about how you define the performance of your school. The most successful organisations use a balanced combination of hard and soft measures.

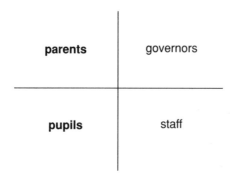

Figure 6.2   The balanced scorecard

Exercise

1. For each of the key 'stakeholder' groups in Figure 6.2 identify a key performance indicator. In other words, to meet your school's strategy/objectives, what does success look like for each group? These may be 'hard' measures such as the numbers of exams passes, or 'softer' ones such as staff morale.
2. For each indicator draw a graph to show the performance trend over the last three years.
3. Now you are in a position to set specific targets/objectives in each area. This 'template' of performance indicators and objective could be the starting point for the school's objective-setting process.

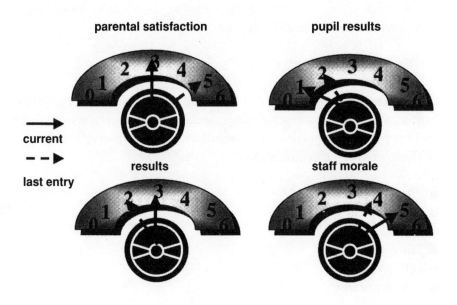

Figure 6.3   A performance 'dashboard' for your school

Many organisations which use balanced scorecards talk about monitoring their performance dashboard. Having correctly identified what makes a difference to each of your stakeholder groups, you can monitor those indicators that will really make a difference in your school's performance.

Two things will be vital to your success

First, you need a clear strategy, otherwise how will you know if you are measuring and managing those things that will help you achieve it?

Second, focus your attention on those things that will actually make a difference to the performance of your school, teachers and pupils. There is always a temptation to measure the things that are easy to measure, whether or not they impact performance. If you do this, remember that you will be focusing attention to something that does not really make a difference.

What gets measured gets done.

Picking the right measures can be a challenge, particularly on the 'softer' side. Using school climate, that is the perceptions of staff and/or pupils about the environment of the school, may help.

These are the key dimensions:

- flexibility;
- responsibility;
- standards;
- rewards;
- clarity;
- commitment.

All these dimensions are measurable by questionnaire and/or through transforminglearning.com.

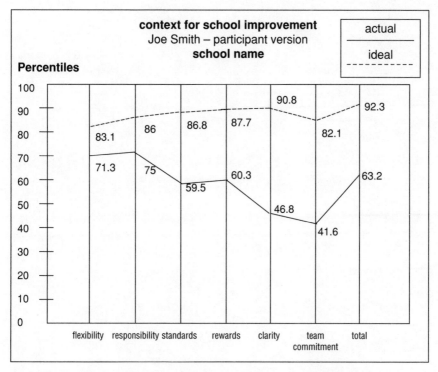

Figure 6.4   The context for school improvement (school climate)

References and further reading

REFERENCES

Covey, S (1992) *The Seven Habits of Highly Successful People*, Simon and Schuster, London

Department for Education and Employment (DfEE) (1998) *Teachers Meeting the Challenge of Change*, Green Paper, DfEE, London, December.

DfEE (2000a) Performance Management in Schools (ref. DFEE 0051/200), *Model Performance Management Policy*, DfEE, London

DfEE (2000b) Research Report RR216, *Research into Teacher Effectiveness* by Hay McBer, DfEE, London, June.

FURTHER READING

Caldwell, B and Spinks J (1998) *Beyond the Self Managing School*, Falmer Press, London

Coupland, D (1991) *Generation X*, Abacus, London

Hartle, F (1997) *Transforming the Performance Management Process*, Kogan Page, London

Hartle, F and Weiss T (1997) *Reengineering Performance Management*, St Lucie Press, Florida

Havard, B (2001) *Performance Appraisals*, Kogan Page, London

Kaplan, R and Norton D (1996) *The Balanced Scorecard*, HBS Press, Harvard University Business School, Cambridge, Mass.

Senge, P (2001) *Schools That Learn*, Nicholas Brealey Publishing, London

Index

Page references in italic indicate tables or figures